Here's Hoping You Never See This

Here's Hoping You Never See This

Emma Bleker

Cover Design by Alyssa Nip

Emma Bleker
2015

First Printing: 2015

ISBN 978-1-329-57004-7

For J and H

Contents

Acknowledgements

A whole world of thanks to all those who have supported and continue to support this journey. Special thanks to Pablo for always reading, Alyssa for sharing her incredible talent with this project, Bailey for all the unwavering support, and Jim, for absolutely everything. To all, thank you for reading.

Here's Hoping You Never See This

Emma Bleker

The Heart Writings, A Manifesto
pt. 1

On Becoming Sand And Growing A New Heart

This place is one of electricity, but also of spilled beer, and I
haven't decided which means more to me. I am picking last
week from my teeth, but I am prone to bleeding. I think part of it
is my mouth warning me to stop letting go of the things it hasn't
yet gotten over. It says to me, "he kissed you last 3 days ago, do
not clean his spit from your mouth. you may never be able to
taste it again", and I wonder if this is the thing that makes it hard
to get out of bed. Everything's lost its flavor anyway so I almost drown
trying to rinse him from my tongue.
I was given instructions on how not to live like this and how not
to love like they did and like I used to and how not to imagine the
waterfront as a resting place. They warn me, the water sneaks up
on those who trust it. I have to remind myself not to identify with the
sand. I was not meant to sleep beneath a great thing, I was meant to be
the great thing. So I dream of the great thing.

I dreamt the sea let me inside of her.
I woke, wet.

I continue to break apart like the sand, but I tell my mother that
nothing particularly interesting happened this week and my sheets
are clean and I am not eating dirt anymore. I do not tell her I am
sleeping on moss and laundry I forgot to fold and I lie about forgetting
to fold the laundry because I know exactly what I am doing and what
I have done and I call it 'forget' but I mean 'help me'.
Each skinned knee has become a shrine to the fall that caused it.
I hate pain and he is so gentle and does not touch me like I am
broken but knows where the cracks are. What I am saying is, he is the
only thing I know how to do right. What I am saying is, I am trying to
be the ocean and I am being absorbed into things that do not know how
to be in their own space. I only want to be something that is not easily
separated from itself; I want to be here without losing myself. How the
sand must miss consistency. How the sand must miss togetherness.

I sleep inside of his warm belly.
I wake, wet.

Reverb

There is a woman walking down the street too late at night,
her skin only apparent to be skin because of the lights, and even then,
they keep sputtering out, so who knows what exactly she is.
A man watches from his balcony as the lights switch off in a
living room, then moments later, on in an upstairs bedroom.
He is almost positive the one doing the moving inside of the house
is human. He cannot be sure, he is only watching.

Something moves in a woman's gut and she thinks to tell the world
that she believes her sadness has grown arms and a head
and fingernails. She is sure it is not human, but it is alive.

I am telling my mother secrets in my empty room, and she will
never hear them. They would make her wonder what I am.
Somewhere, something sounds wrong, and nowhere looks like
a place we used to frequent when we were trying so hard
to fit into different skin that our own somehow became unfamiliar.
The woman on the phone tells someone on the other line that she
is fine and a man listening nearby suppresses the urge to engulf her,
to embrace her until she is gone, until they are both gone.
He does not look up from his book, but he feels as if he is
fighting to keep today's breakfast in his body, he feels like the
world is turning upside down and he is holding on without moving
from his place, all the while something is being stolen from them both.

The dark earth is a mighty breath in tonight, as we suspect we may
be alien. Somewhere, it is quiet, and nothing is being disturbed.
Somewhere, no one is screaming. I am deep inside this
thing I am, whatever that may be, wondering how to be so that I may
be perceived as in a place I may belong.

There is a distant smell of smoke.
Somewhere that is not where I am,
someone else wonders who it is,
this time, too.

Buried Things Being Flooded Back to the Ground

This body has walls like old wood
and in the middle of the night,
moans are mistaken for
footsteps. There is no other way.
Everyone who sleeps in this bed
is sure that it is haunted. I do not
have the heart to tell them they are
sleeping in a graveyard. I do not
have the right body to tell them
not to be afraid. I do not have the
heart to tell them that I am not
haunted, but inhabited. They
do not attempt to hide themselves
anymore. They walk the hallways
and scream in my ears. They stand
before me, bleeding.

The Great Fall

Like rain to its
ocean, you have
seamlessly
become part of
me.

Wanting

I wake up each
morning wanting
more of you.

First, it was your
lips, then it was
your hands, now
it is your heart.

Now, it is always
your heart.

If It Will Not Go, Invite It Inside, Keep It Warm

Tremendous hurt does not
leave you. It stays inside,
planted; the one thing that
will always stay. The
tumor that cannot be cut
around. Do not work to
kill the unkillable thing,
give it companionship. Let
it know your love. Then,
see how it can transform.
Never gone, but with the
chance to change. A pain
given purpose through light.

When It Calls Home To Check-In and You Cannot Pick Up The Phone

I am a heart buried by
its own beating.

Have you ever seen a
thing gnaw into itself
until it can no longer
bare the same name?

Have you ever
seen a thing wish so
desperately to
know itself, that it
becomes something
else entirely?

3am On The Closet Floor, A Love Letter to Old Sadness

The bottom of the bath tub looks
lonely so I do not drown it and I sit
with her all night and it is not for
me, I tell the water, it is not for me.

There is blood on the bed but we
forgot how to talk about the things
that make us bleed and we go for
a drive and we do not ask for
directions because it has always
been difficult to ask how not to drive
off the cliff and we get lost, every time.

There is rhythm to this loneliness.
There is rhythm and familiarity
where the floor of the closet meets
the tremor body of the translucent
girl. And we hear them whisper,
"we know this."

We hear ourselves whisper,
"how can we live any differently?
has anyone ever lived any
differently?"

Holding Funerals for Those Who Have Not Yet Died

Even after they find him, and even
after we know he's never going to
breathe again, and even after
something within me begins to
die, I am thinking about what I will
make for breakfast and if my
mother is thinking about her mother
and I am trying to remember the
smell of freshly peeled oranges but
the memories are coming out
rotten. It will be days before I wake
up. It will be days before the smoke
leaves the kitchen. When you find
it in yourself to look at the concrete
on the highway and think of something
that is not roadkill, you will know
the day is over. You will know the
searching is done.

Emerging, And Explaining The Wet Clothes To Loved Ones

Her goodbyes will
start out baring a striking
resemblance to "come back."

Give the skin time
to recognize itself.
For those whose
heads have been
held under water,
the ocean does
not seem to be a
gentle thing.

She will question
the sanctity of the
serenity.

She will distrust
the easy rocking of
your bodies; it will
remind her of a
sickness.

The goodbyes will
evolve, the heart is not
naive. But do not wait
for her to subside.

She is not a storm
to wait out.

Defacing Graveyards

The haunting was not slow, nor menacing, simply something we
were born knowing we would have to live with. It was a birth mark,
a deformity so defective it was unseeable, a wound like milk spilled on
the kitchen floor. An inconvenience no one would take credit for
creating, that was not spoken of, but sat with us at dinner and crawled
through my clothes each morning before I told them I loved them.

As children, it was bodies in the doorway and the nights spent squeezing
our knees to our chests so hard we thought we may grow smaller
until there was no smaller to grow and how wild, we thought,
how wild that we were finally able to breathe. As adults, we found
lovers and left lovers and did not let ourselves stay long enough to
be left by lovers and salty skin was a good reminder that the body
can be bitter.

We left sheets tangled, like restraints. We looked back and thought,
'i am too aware to hold myself prisoner.' As adults, it was the bed,
always too big for our bodies, and the sunlight come early
to rip us from the sleep that had only come so soon before.

It began to know us. The home began to smell of burning hair and
the nights we did not sleep and the sheets we could not make ourselves
wash. The air was a choking, spurting gargle of a last breath,
every moment filled with the emptiness of, "i wish i had called my
parents back yesterday" and "if i die today, my roommate will find
vomit in the toilet and i will not be there to hide in my room
so i do not have to apologize" and "i'm sorry i gave your
favorite poem to someone else when i was trying to tell them i loved
them, i didn't know that you had the same intention
when you first shared it with me."

As we are now, we are followed, as each person is by their own rot.
As we are now, we are entirely surrounded by ourselves, this foreign
entity. Each haunting is its own, but exists intimately to itself.

What else would stay with us for so long, if not the shadows
of our own doings?

Necessary Ingredients

When she calls him 'honey,'
she is making a choice.
Behind the sweetness of the
thing are hundreds of tiny
working pieces: the hive, full;
the home, him; the heart,
them. She puts him in
everything, and everything
is sweet because of it.

On Nights Like These When We Cannot Get Warm

On some kind of a night that does not
seem to be a special kind of night,
the moon looks to swallow and the
girl looks to be tended to. It is often
like this. She scales the sides of
buildings and cuts her legs on rusted
nails, those things that will not
cling to her, but reach for her, beg
her to dig herself into them until
they bleed. Until they both bleed.
Until the sky bleeds. And so, parched,
the moon watches. Reaching, the
moon begs to be touched by the
sharp fingers of the punctured sky.
The sky the girl climbs to, wishing
to be punctured by.

Entire and Complete

The ash in her hair lends itself
to my imagination, burning
backwards into a cigarette or
a fireplace or the hands of
a man who cannot help but
fall apart against her; burning
backward into all the pieces
of things we are told were
born whole. We never could
imagine them whole.

It's Nothing New, Really.

Strawberries rot if
left pressed up
against one another
for too long.

It does not mean
you have done
anything wrong.

I thought about
telling you this
the last time I
saw you.

Even sweet things
can find their end,
in the rot.

Each thing takes
its own time to
become unsalvageable.

They've Been Using Their Teeth

I am learning to swallow the good things. I pretend the dead do not live inside of me. Scratch that. I pretend the dead really are dead, I pretend they do not reside in the trees or in the fabric of my sheets. I pretend I do not miss being able to believe in a god.

I do not answer your phone calls anymore. They feel too much like closing my eyes in a cemetery at night, like letting go of the steering wheel at 86 miles an hour on the highway. Everyone can see them, anyway, and I worry sometimes that mouths like the ones I keep encountering tell stories to one another's eyes. I worry they think these wounds are getting old. I could have told them this. It's like cutting into a corpse, sometimes. They just won't close.

I am in love with a boy I could bathe in the thought of. I dream these hands together, wrapped up in one another until the only thing left between our bodies is the promise of stories I will one day tell him. I could listen to him speak until my ears curl up around all the things he means to say, has ever meant to have said. I am trying to love myself better. He is helping.

My friends are dying and I don't know what to say to their parents. She used a rope. All I can think about is her little brother.

I am learning how to grow up, but my god, it rips me apart. I don't know how to un-see the hurting. I don't know how to call my mother without crying.

Stepping Inside

You described yourself
as a burning house, so
I climbed inside.

I sucked your smoke
in through my nose and
told you I breathed
better, here.

You opened all the
windows, but I could
tell the effort made
your shoulders heavy.
I said, "Close them all,
I'll be just fine."

It was impossible to
suffocate inside of you;
I have never met a body
so similar to my own.

What better place for a
burning girl than the floor
of something like a burning world?

Wonder How

You have sheets on your bed
that still smell like her, but you
hid the letters and called it
moving on, so when your friends
ask, you tell them it is midnight,
it is always midnight, and the
sun has forgotten how to spell
your name. This is how they
know she has not called you.

On a rainy Tuesday in November,
Mercury is in retrograde and for
a moment the blood inside of
you stands still. The light is
bearable again and all the colors
on your skin agree to stop fighting
for just a little while. You read an
article that told you not to make
agreements when the cosmos
are given permission to reach out
to our bodies; your body goes
back to war, it is once again
impossible to sleep. You miss the
sky that you found in her palms.

For three months straight, you
have ordered insignificant items
to be delivered to your house.

Every time there is a knock on
the door, your body feels like it
has come alive, the image of her,
smiling, blinds you. She is never
the one knocking. Everyone says
you are doing this to yourself.

We Unlearned the Drowning Together

I did not know how to
love this ocean of a
body until I was taught
how to swim.

Toothpicks

I tend to pull at the loose parts of myself until I come undone, I often come undone. It happens in the strangest of places; public bathrooms, my mother's kitchen, in the mouth of a boy I have not thought of for months. He still keeps me between his teeth, I know, because I can feel the splinters in my sides from time to time.

I am thinking of a way to tell you something to which I cannot put words. I have never been able to craft bodies for the things I most wish to give away. I hope you'll settle for a gift-wrapped box and a handwritten letter. I still haven't decided what I am putting in it. I have not decided if it is better to leave the letter empty.

Someone once told me that the stars see what we need, and react accordingly. Now, watching them with you, I feel as if they watch me too. It would be so much less lonely, here. It is getting so much less lonely, here.

On Finding Comfort in New Names

If there is no end, there are infinite possible universes
in which we are all, potentially, so much happier.

Infinite spaces in which the someone you love builds
monuments to you, monuments that look like coffee in the
morning and fingers folded into one another on the long
drive home; a whole universe dedicated to the happiest day
of your life, and the lives of all those you keep within you, and
all the days they did not survive to see.

In some universe, you wake up each morning in my arms
and wrap yourself around me like you never left, because
here, you never did. In another, we were born an
ocean away from one another and both of us failed to
cross it. I do not hurt for the loss of that
which I never yearned for.

Knowing what I know,
I would choose the latter,
every time.

There is a name hidden beneath my heart. It has not
lived there for long, but it has begun to grow inside of
me, wrapping its soft limbs around my most fragile
pieces. Somewhere, I do not fear this engulfment.

I swear I can hear it kneading away at the
knots you left me in. In some place, I am not
begging to be loved by something that does
not wish to steal me from myself.

There is a world in which I am
worth something
more
than what you made of me.

I Am Trying To Put It Into Words

I say that I love every part of you, knowing precisely
what it is I mean to say. "I love every part of you",
as in "I know I haven't seen every part of you, but I know
I will love them, when I finally meet them."

As in, "I know your heart can get messy sometimes.
I know, because mine can, too. I am good at holding things
as they fall apart. It is all soft palms, here. It is
the kind of holding that is supported by shaking
knees, but does not, itself, waver.

I will help you pick up the pieces, every time, if you'll
have me; if having those shards of you recovered is
the thing you need from this space we share."

As in, "I know you will inevitably say hurtful things,
and I know you will not mean them. I know I
will not always be easy to love, and I'm not sure
I know how to tell you that
I want everything you are."

As in, "I will not let you be the only one left. I will
be there to listen to you, even when I don't understand
you. I keep saying that stars seem to be living beneath
your skin, and I want nothing more than to fall
further into your sky."

I say that I love every part of you, knowing precisely
what it is I meant to say.

I love all your past and all of your tomorrow; I
love the sky inside your heart, in all its infinite light.

I love you, whole.
Every single star.

On Being Ocean, As Human

Know the body you swim within.
Open your eyes, even when it stings.
The things you will see; oh, the
things you will see.
The unhumanness you will discover
will threaten to drown you.
This depth is terrifying.

When He Tells You He Still Has Your Name Spelled In Glow-In-The-Dark Stickers On His Ceiling, Do Not Think It Romantic

I know he is trying to say,
"I still think of you every
night before I fall asleep."

I know he cannot find the
heart to tell me that I still
light up his room.

I know he does not want
to hurt me, and so he does
not tell me that the glow,
the slight pulse of me
is the reason he can no
longer sleep through
the night.

I know he does not like
seeing me cry, and so he
cannot tell me how he
keeps the lights on when
he fucks her so he is not
tempted to tear me down,

off the wall,

out of his head.

The Someday Place

We seek to escape the
'someday' that lasts
forever, and yet we etch
ourselves into stone
and say, 'here, now we
will know that we were
once young in this place.'

We seek to escape this
place of 'one day,' while
we bathe in it, and bask
in its heart, and beg it
to keep us."

Apologies I've Come From
pt. 2

This Is What It Means

We go back to the corner where we first began the process of
growing ourselves and touch the concrete that now sits in place
of the flower bed we took the soil from. We call the new thing
beautiful, even though we are both thinking "destroyer" and
go on our way. We do not call old flames. We do not crawl in
the windows of old friends, or climb up next to them in bed,
or ask if they miss it as much as we do.

Another boy from our graduating class dies and we research
it on the internet for 3 whole days. We do not sleep, but we
know the police report a little too well (we burned it into the
insides of our eyelids for comfort,) but when our parents ask
we say we didn't know him and we say we'll ask our friends
if they know what happened and the door shuts and we
act like home is still the place we grew up and it isn't as easy
as we think it would be.

We run into a boy we think we once loved and there is a
kind of drowned wanting between us, because we are not
what the other needs anymore, and it's sad because both of us
know there's nothing left and it's all dried up; but seeing each
other reminds us both that there was a time when we were
all but immortalized by refusing to believe we would ever
not be young, and it should have been easiest to love another
person then, but we were selfish and small and unmade
and there is something empty
about that.

This is the story. We go back to the things we once
called "now". We go back, and we go back, and we
try to stay. We always try to stay.

Lessons In Opposites

New like, "touch me"
Old like, "my skin still wakes up when you touch me"

Win like, "convince myself i have changed their mind"
Lose like, "this will not stop unless i succumb"

Love like, "stay a few minutes"
Fuck like, "gone before either has (is) finished"

Present like, "your body is full of reverberation, cling to me"
Absent like, "i was gone while you came"

Hard like, "i haven't seen you in days and i forgot to notice"
Easy like, "you are the one thing i do not plan on"

Desert like, "nothing to do but die together of dehydration"
Ocean like, "enveloped by you; wet, wet, wet"

Beginning like, "i know exactly what this is and what the fuck is this"
End like, "never seen, only collided with."

A Poem Called Body

This poem squirms within its shape.

Do not imagine the poem a woman.

In the bedroom, there is kept an
arsenal of love letters; this poem
is eager for the day they are
burned alive. The woman knows
she will be the one to kill them.

She felt most at home under the
nails of past lovers, she has since
been washed away. The poem only
wishes it could bleed. It rips itself
open in its yearning and still,
nothing.

The woman cannot remember her name.

Who does not imagine the woman, a poem?

The Great Collapse

I made from our ruins, a monument;
a reminder to myself
that worship does not keep
temples from falling apart.

Laundry Day

I fold myself into the pages of his palms
I am left in the back pocket of the jeans he wears when all his other
clothes are dirty
I am left there when he takes his clothes to the wash
I am broken down and
I am flimsy and
I am easily pulled apart
I become the thing he wonders about when he pulls his jeans out from
the machine
I am nothing, nothing is left, but the thing he feels sadness for having
lost but
I am not me, to him - he has forgotten what he placed there
I am a forgotten thing he misses out of instinct
I am still dissolved and
I am still undone but
I am missed and
I am wondered about and
he is momentarily bothered because he cannot place the image
of me and he is sad
before he forgets that I was even a consideration and
that is enough.
I promise that is enough.

Where It Lives

I am hanging on a clothesline somewhere in Texas where they still use
clotheslines and I can hear my mother singing from back when she was
sixteen, climbing out the window to the background noise of her mother
refusing to unlock the bathroom door, and all the while I am stuck too
close to the ground for my suspension to feel anything but hopeless, eternal.

I heard they re-wrote yesterday and the week before and in a year
we will not remember that they told us it happened differently than it
did - because there will be new yesterdays to be looking back on.
And in a year we will not remember that we questioned how they
could justify not calling those things they say did not happen, fires.
People who placed the value of car windows above the value of
beating hearts. There will be new outrage and all behind us, fires.

Part of me is melted into a Texas sidewalk traveled upon by men
who do not like to listen when their daughters tell them that the boy
next door is trying to make basins of their bodies. One man in particular, he
picks vernacular from his teeth, says it is his right to step, as hard as he
would like. He does not speak quietly when he turns the bodies of those
I grew up beside into lessons for his sons.

In this town, I am a structure of barbed wire imitating a human being,
a stick pin promise you asked never to come back; but I did, and if we're
being honest, which we aren't, necessarily: it's hard to commit to becoming
the storm by reminding them that I always will, every time I have the chance.
Because sometimes, I won't. But I try not to tell them that. I try to keep
quiet and ask about their children's schooling and talk about how the town
looks a little different and no matter how much they tell me that nothing
has changed, I seem to know. I think I scare them.

The water we played in as children or young adults or those who birth trouble
or whatever they called us to keep from calling us human, that water is
boiling. They invite us from dry land, in the comfort of dry clothes, on the
other side, to swim. "Get in," they say, "come in, it is so nice."

I Did Not Think I Would Miss Being Away So Badly

She tells me of the non-love
and I see the monster of my
parents: Coal on dry ice skin;
Two kinds of burn.

The season changes and I am
asked if I remember the name
of the first. I tell them no and
taste the blood in my mouth
beginning to well.

I sit alone in a restaurant and
write a poem to keep from
catching the looks people give
to those who eat alone in
restaurants.

The boy I love has every piece
of my heart, except for the
ones I lost before knowing him.
We share what is left.

It is a birthday party and I am
the confetti left on the kitchen
floor that no one wants to
clean up. They used to love
all the color, now it is only mess.

I eat gingerbread pancakes and
pretend my phone is not dead.
This is how we survive.
By pretending there is someone
on the other line.

It Is Suddenly Too Clear That We Still Live

We lock the doors and we are fine but when people call
we say we are not feeling well and we look up pictures
and we cry over the pictures and we can't breathe through
our noses but it isn't about us, and that
is hard to remember.

When the boy dies, we think about our boyfriends and
our brothers and our friends and when the second boy dies
we think about ourselves and tomorrow and we wish
we could just hold everyone we love against us until
they are
old enough to die.

No one is ever old enough to die, but there is something
haunted about a life ending before it has been lived and
it is hard not to stay inside all day because somewhere
in our minds we think the outside killed them but
we know all too well that inside kills too
so we go on with our lives but
there is so much fear.

We look at the last picture he posted on Facebook
and we screenshot his last tweet and it says something like
"fuck this cold weather shit" and we are wondering if it meant
anything more but we know it didn't.

We look at pictures of his girlfriend and we wonder if
she will ever smile like she did when she was with him
and she probably will but my god she's probably sobbing on
her closet floor and my body aches to think of the way she must
be moaning, that pointless begging into the nothing,
that fruitless
wailing.

We cannot stop thinking
about the wailing.

Making Wicked The Thing You Yearn For

Something sounds like
what we used to suspect home might sound like.
It is something like knocking.
Just a little sound.
It reaches into the place
behind your heart and opens itself up.
I turn down the music and make
all of it quiet, all the noise soft.
Now, it goes with the things
that distract me from it.
We bandage our broken limbs and walk
on them like everything is fine,
but every step is, still, like crunching
bones, and we can hear them now.
This is the way it makes you feel -
like you could find the thing
you are meant to love simply by
silencing everything else.
This is how you are made to feel -
as if the masked thing reaching
for you knows your name
better as a taste between its teeth.

With These Hands

A cold, brass bar wills itself into the gut of the
heart of a girl too far past herself to recognize
the intruder as foreign; the cold thing seems to be
nothing new, nothing particularly new.

A woman's flower garden goes gray and nothing
can bring it back to life. The woman moves
homes and stops planting flowers and
finds something underneath her chest that
was left too long to be recognizable.
The things that have been buried come back
to ask her where she's been.

A sound comes from beneath
the dirt, and we think of all those
things we have buried,
what could be calling for us.
We think of the cold things still
sleeping inside of us.

It is nothing all too new,
nothing particularly new.

I Don't Believe In god But I Always Thought I'd End Up In The Sky

We became estranged from
ourselves the day the stars
fell. Why would they throw
themselves from the very
place we had always hoped
to ascend?

Waking Up As My Father's Daughter

I am told there is something that feels like the sun in the summer
within a red cup and I am asked to see how my name sounds
at the bottom of it. When I find it, it looks familiar, like a
dead animal on the back porch.

And I learn how I am meant to die.

I am meant to die of thirst. I am meant to die thirsty.
I am meant to fall in love with swallowing until I am drowned.

In my blood is a disease my body decided I did not need the
company of, but left the shadow; left the haunt.
I worry for my one day daughter, I worry for my one day son;
that they may be possessed by the dormant
death inside of me.

This is what it means to call yourself 'daughter.'
This is the meaning of inheritance, and of family, and of doom.

We will call this next part 'sister.'
She is wild and alien and her heart is solid, crystalline … ex-pensive …

She is full of drink and she sways like a broken sailboat going
home to its ocean. It is not yet sinking. It has been doing
this for years. It is whole, believing it will never come to
the end. It says it knows what it is doing.
I see the motions stained into her clothing: "i will not die the
way he did," (I worry too often she will die the way he did)
as she nurses sharp breath, nurtured like a parched child.
This mouth has been tended to, she has made sure of it.

It has been nurtured, with great care, spitting as she tumbles,
barefoot, above his grave. Above his lingering "i'm sorry, i'm sorry, i'm sorry."

She still writes him letters.
She still fights with him as if she could win. She still runs to the
edge of the water and thinks, affectionately, about the pop of
her ears and the surge of water into her lungs; about the sinking.
She still thinks about joining him on the bottom of the ocean.

This is what is means to be his daughter. This ache of re-living the

watching. And we did so much watching: as he
became himself, submerged.

This suicide was a complicated one.

The kind where you know the slow death is looming but no one
wants to ask the sick person with the sour breath just how
long they will let themselves live and so they have a drink at dinner
and they say it is not so bad anymore and we take one day off
the calendar and keep coming back each night, as if
he loves us enough to stay.

And we question it, 'why did he not love us enough to stay?
why did he hold such space in his heart for the thing he
would die for?'

And, always, 'was he further in love with his sickness than with us, the
things he gave it to? but he loved us enough to give us that thing that
consumed his life and so he gave us everything.'

I take this knowledge, his death note, this certificate of no more,
and wrap it around my neck.

This is what it means to be
his daughter.

This is what it means to keep myself from becoming one who
cannot help but die, one who is like his sick knees and
sore skin. This is my sickness: the sickness of worry for those with
blood like mine. The sickness of worry for those who
would die for the thing I watched kill.

And here in the end, you sit awake at night thinking "how can the
body be 65% water if all you take into yourself is guilt, if it is the only
thing that quenches you? if you are the only one with your blood
who cannot call this thing your own?"

This is what it means to be his daughter:
To love what is gone.
To hold regret, like a newborn, gently, for
having to love in spite of something.

Unnamed

maybe it's my fault for bleeding so much or maybe i was made to be recognized as sister by the knife but somewhere there is a boy trying to bury his weapon, trying to bury his hands, and somewhere he is asking for pity because he cannot seem to rinse me from his skin.

On Nights When You Fear You Have Become The Burden, And The Music Doesn't Settle Right

When it happens at a party and you are supposed to smile
and you have a beer in each hand, the inside of your
conversation partner's mouth will grow until you are trapped
inside of it. You will shrink until you are
shaking inside of it.

You will not be able to open your eyes. You will not be able
to convince yourself that you are still alive.

There is something without a name crawling under your skirt,
and it bites; your teeth will tell you to run. Or, that is to say,
the canopy will come down even if you have spent your
fifteen years or nineteen years or thirty seven years
hammering it into the earth. That is to say, the earth
will never be dry. That is
to say, the sky is always trying
to flood us.

The water is always trying to
become us.

You will be denied the space in your body when the air in
the room goes without warning you. It will all be empty and
something will fill your ears.

Here, the sky opens up: at a house party on a Saturday
night. In the middle of the woods. On the back of the one who
carries it. In the mouth of the corpse. At the bottom of your cup.

You are not hearing
what you think you are
hearing.

You have not become what the thing around
your ankles scratches
into your skin.

With Care

Hand-drawn is the body of the woman,
pulsing: the ink so like blood, those
watching find no comfort.
The body too like a woman, those
watching have their comfort taken from their hands.

When fingers try to make a woman,
they end mostly in fire. Mostly it is all fire.

Somewhere under a house that used
to have a name, a living thing tries to
convince itself of its body;
a living thing tries to convince
itself that it is not just and only body.

More frightful than the form,
the thing that turns them away,
is that which makes them turn.

Hot steel, sweltering metallic blood;
she is the trapped moan
under the tongue that begs itself
free.

We are made to avert
our eyes, for how we recognize
ourselves in the stroke of her.

She is too like us
for there to be any
comfort.

We recognize that
red.

To, And In, And From, And For

She has spent this time breaking it away,
and it comes off easy, like the old familiar moan they used
to call her home; bleeds only because she is told it will
make people believe her to be human.

We are all only trying to convince those who
would not ask
that we are human.

We only ask for people
without names to be called by.

This is the kind of cry no one can hear:
the scratching down the walls that
seeks to warn you that it remains,
haunting, for you.

Those who hear its lingering only wish
to be distinguished from it; we only
wish to say, we are not like the dead. We
are not like the haunting.

In this way, we are called home.

Stuck In The Throat

A woman stands before the ocean's mouth,
upon the water's tongue.

There is a sameness, standing with toes
testing the ocean's reach, a kind of desperation for her touch,
dripping with caution for risk of being drowned:

To come to oneself, as the ocean comes
to itself.

To force yourself away so that you may
come back, fuller.

Opened up, laid out: from the ocean she learned,
she must force away the thing that makes her full
until she is stretched out, until she is
reaching so far she is called mighty.

This is her envy:
that coming to and going from, that rhythmic
heartbeat. The part that makes it beautiful, the waves:
the only way to keep yourself is to beat what
is inside of you until it is soft.

She takes the body of the sea, she sees
herself in the bottom of her own belly and
asks the surge to give her leave to be empty.

She begs her body to contain its tide.

Purge becomes an ocean word.
The motion of the away, a function of her beauty.

What a Thing Is

She was not a glass box, nor a scream in an empty home.

She was not knocking on the front door but
she looked similar to the sound of it.
Where there is a noise that sounds like
bells, she is not thought of.

Her skin was not unlike gravel roadways, but not
like it either; her insides, not so like carnival rides.

She was not broken fingernails, though they were of her.

She was not milk dripping from the chin of an
overeager face; she was not the lapping up of
spilled-over mess; she did not lie below the overeager
mouth. Her mouth was never anything but
a mouth.

She was not repellant, and just the same, she was not loved.

Her smile was not a bridge or the water below it,
or the tremor of the body earth, or the bottom of the
heavy thing that walks upon its own skin.
She was not explosive, not a flat tire
or a warm bed.

The things living inside of her did not bother
with putting their teeth away.

She was not hungry, but
swallowed and kept, and kept,
and kept.
She was not full.

She was not able
to keep.

What We Might See, This Time

When it comes in waves, when it comes in great
moments, the collision does not seem so colossal.

The great surge of the impact is worth the pieces lost.
There are no great silent days of mourning for the
way the sand is thrown until it succumbs to the smallness.
You learn early, people cannot turn away
from the circus of a crash.

There is a man with freshly cut hair, pin-sized
shavings missed by the hairdresser still clinging
to the pricked skin on the back of his neck;
pieces let go which still hold on.

There is no way to miss a thing if losing it
makes you lighter.

Your body comes, made from nails,
and I had only wanted to be warm today.
I am unraveled, the floor is covered.

She is alone in a room, a room made to look
like it is for sleeping. She is in darkness,
like burial, all ash and soot lighting to
calm the burning bed frame.

No one waits for someone to come home.

We pretend we are not waiting
for someone to come home.

It is not meant to convince. The pieces lost in the
waiting, sprawled out before the waves: a sacrifice.

An offering to the ocean,
that we, too, crash.

The Summer Of Big Chew And Sleeping Inside Of Playground Slides

Before the winter took hold of this town,
back before we lost
her long hair, the something beneath the skin that seemed
to be of the sun, the pieces of us picked away
Like old wounds clawed back to healed surface,
there is a conversation in which nothing is said
conducted in a room in which there is no space
upon the back of an idea that has not the capacity to carry.

There is coldness that feels like ice and then
there is coldness that feels like saying goodbye
to your mother for the first time.

Outside, the air is full of neither.

When the gates were still open, before the apple tree fell
into the great big home on the corner with the green window shades,
Like an invitation come too late,
there is a man with a suit two sizes too big walking
down a street that does not seem to be different from
the other streets, toward a house that is too new to be called a home,
with a girl inside who has just taken scissors to her girlish hair:
her bathroom floor a massacre of brown strands and pink lipstick
smeared over like blood stains.

There is a place past the house that looks
like its belly is empty. When the lights do not
turn on, back when the lights did not turn
on, they slept inside these fixtures.

There is a girl curled into
the half-moon of a boy's body.

Inside, the air smells of bubble gum and manure.

Back before the place was gone to itself,

back before we lost
the image of a girl sneaking into her window on the second floor,
scaling the side of the house in a pink dress, the part of us
that didn't know how to clean blood stains from the kitchen
floor before company came,

Like setting the table was foreign preparation,
in a house that would soon no longer be a house
within a moment that would not be remembered by any but those who
were there
a baby girl is born, as a car collides with a
stop sign.

Snowmen Kept Alive By The Freezer

Ten-year-old boys with big hearts do not
let go of homemade things so easily.
He seems to be made of something that goes
untouchable, the remnants of a familiarity
we sacrificed for something else.
What had seemed to be more important,
we could not tell you.

The way there is a driveway parade each time
a gone thing comes home, the day he
let the snowman live, the apprehension of those
who knew that snowmen were meant to melt
hung low and heavy like fog clinging to the wet grass.
The welcome was purely his own.

It is hard for people to watch
something hopeful keep alive a thing
that is meant to be forgotten.
The home was made, and the home was kept.

Until May, when it was so oddly misplaced,
no one could stand to question it anymore.
Until May, when it grew to be part of the metal
wire shelf – when it made company of the
vodka bottles and air-tight packaged meat
and the rest of the lingering that told stories of our home.

We put things in the freezer to keep them
from rotting before we need them,
or to keep them from going stale before we
need them, and we think he stayed because
something in us would never need him, but
knew there was comfort in being able to say
that he was there.

This is the way we were taught to keep:
without talking about the ways we could be lost.

Watching The Sun Set From The Surface Of The Room

To make a thrashing thing still,
you do not smother it.
You do not tell it, 'bodies do
not move like that.'
It will begin to think itself
unnatural. An alienated thing
cannot be expected to know
that it is human.

August, a Ghost Story

Small voices come from
the trees, like rain to feed
the grass. Wings outstretched
to find the wind, companion,
against their tiny chests.

The bones of a bird
make them their most
fragile and, in the same
gust, allow them to
fly.

The bones of a bird
know what it means
to question
what you are.

Outstretched, like the sky
will only take them if they
are open. This is the way
a fragile thing moves.

Their voices fall
like the rest
before them
                    and
        where
                do they
                land?

Small, beating hearts,
glowing above us:
another kind of sunshine.

This is the way a fragile thing moves.

And when we find its body,

a cold, huddled intrusion
to the litter and tire tracks
in the parking lot
behind the
7-Eleven,
we wonder if anyone else
notices how empty the sky feels.

We wonder how we could have
failed to notice the sound,
gone quiet,
and the ground,
gone dry.

Taking a Walk Past Midnight, Or My First Attempt At Dying

From my mother, I inherited this troubled prickling
beneath the skin and my strong legs and my big cheeks
and, I suspect, the thing that makes you heavy, tries to
convince you that you are alone and will not come out
from under whatever is suffocating you, no matter how
hard you try; tries to convince you that it is more
alive than you have ever been. We are such like women.

She told me once, living in New York City, of running
through the 3:00 am minefield barefoot with a bat
in her hand. I fear for the woman I know survived.
I fear for her bloody feet and I worry for her heart,
tripping over every clamor her breath made in the dark.

And they will say, "it is so like a woman, to fear
that which is safe. to worry for the thing you know
made it out alive." And I wonder what did not.
I wonder, I yearn, for that which did not survive
within her. I fear for myself, wonder if I survived.

Where It Comes To Die

In the beginning of this; in the middle of the ocean,
before the exile; I was without and I was breathing.
Neither knew the other.

This will be no surprise: the end will come
at the bottom of a sea. This will be no surprise:
there were things that came before.

Morning, and the eyes open.
A room flooded with light, the kind of
warmth that hums, the kind of thing that
seems to be alive and crawls up from
the end of the bed to catch its inhabitant
in its mouth.

The next day, the sun stays in.
The next day, a young girl stops crying.
The next day, a young girl is buried.

At this burial, a boy sings a song he learned the night before.
The girl's parents cry. They do not hear the song.
The sun comes back home and apologizes for the
worry it has caused, it does not understand why the girl
does not come out to play.

The bed is wet, the mother drowns, and an hour later,
gets up to go to work.

Two years away, a different bed is wet from a
different kind of thing. The blinds are closed
but the windows are open, and the howling is a
kind of third voice in all the holding.

A boy catches his breath, a girl hangs on,
waiting to be caught on his breath.
The body breaks and the bed goes quiet.
The air means to remind of moments come before.

The next day, the bed is half-empty.
The next day, a young girl cries.
Three years later, a key once used by the
boy is melted down to make something
new.

When the breath hitches, like home-made
sweater to rusty nail, I say, I am full of
nails, all around. I say, the bottom of the
ocean is full of sharp unknown.

Nighttime,
an ocean below and above us.
The stars do not fall, for we do not
fear being smothered, but they reach,
like their arms could somehow
find us.

A man three states away drowns.
He is found with your letters down
his throat, and we wonder which
took him first.

We do not attend his funeral,
but watch it on the television.
We stand in the rain,
and ask it to show us:
what was it like to end,
full of something?
What was it like to
sink, knowing it was
all just too heavy?

How else are we meant to
end, we wonder.
How else is the heavy
heart meant to die, but
by sinking?

The Walk

We are somewhere past the last street,
on the last night, in the last town,
or somewhere that feels as though we are,
and all we know is we are not drowning
and we are not speaking.

Street lights bare down, like watching eyes,
threatening to leave our bodies alone
in the dark, in the empty.
Here, we are bound to
be seen.

The boy in the yellow shirt
walks like there is all the room in the world.
I am standing on the edge of
what is an ending world.

Somewhere in her pocket, a kind of
something weighs heavy, a mountain
the size of a thimble.
We do not know how to tell one
another that this place is not
ours.

No one speaks, but the boy picks
at his stained teeth, like he will
find something he lost, like he will
find the day he stopped worrying
that there was ground before him
prior to taking a step.

The girl has dirty fingernails she does
not plan to clean.
She walks like she is going backward,
anomaly in her step.
Some bits of her clothing are torn off,

like she spends her time intimate
with sharp objects. A friend to the
thorns that dress roses.

The open street, to her, must
feel like such a danger: surrounded
only by this air.

The open street, to him: a beacon.

I have no place to walk but forward,
into this nothing gone home to the familiar.

And to me, this place is
nothing but pavement.
Nothing but dirty dishes left
in the sink 3 days too long.
Nothing but the rest of my life.

We each step like we must:
alone to our own movements.

The Way We Tell the Story

I try to tell you what the train between god and a
6th street apartment sounds like and you cannot
take your earphones out long enough
to learn my name.
You never find out where the train
goes to, but you wait for it for
so long, and the trick is, I never
said it was meant to go, at all.
It is past nine, and a man I do not know asks me
to light his cigarette. Two years later, he is hit
by a car. I did not light his cigarette.
I have nightmares about this some nights.
An eye that has swollen itself purple tries to
hide, but is too much like us to go unnoticed.
The music gets louder and the room stops
asking us to dance. The thing we do not remember
to say, is, "have a good day," and "be kind
to yourself," and isn't it funny that
those things are like water, here?
Isn't it funny that we have such
dry throats, here? And these are
the things we choose to forget?
I try to tell you how fast the train
between a body's most vulnerable
soft place and the tip of the knife
goes, but you do not like this story,
you ask me to tell you a different one.
You assume the knife is going for
the body. Everyone assumes the knife
is going for the body. And we tell
another story. We call the knives
something else; we call the knives
'hands' and surrounding us, eyes
welled with waiting and longing turn
to passionate swell as they beg from
us, "And what of the body, moving
toward the hands? What then?"

Opened

In the one word
will live a world:
a world with
people like us,
or, people who are
somehow more like
us than we are.
A world
with dirty dishes
and warm hands.
A beautiful
world.
One that gets
beneath the skin
when we are dreaming
and reminds us of
the place in which
we cannot believe
we already live.
When they say,
"You are safe,"
we believe them.
We see our world.
We walk into it,
eyes burning open.

When Driving Past Homes We Used to Inhabit

To burn down a house, you let it be.
Is this not a comfort?
To water a garden, you use your hands.
But what of the water?
And what of the ground?
To stop a body from bleeding out,
you smother the place of weakness.
And what of the heart?
Does it stop itself from pumping,
does it know it helps the death
come more quickly?
To love another, you must have once been young.
And what of the hands?
To die, you must have once been living.
What is there, here , to hold?

The History of Kissing

Teeth have no place in kissing, and yet,
those accidental, clumsy collisions
will never die completely.
This is something we
know the minute it happens
for the first time.

No matter how many times you have
taken off your shirt for someone
new or bit your lip to draw
them in - teeth used
in a way that is acceptable -
the grind of bone in the
midst of the heat will
take you by surprise, each time.

We either laugh and take it in the
stride of tongue and pull and
grasping bodies, or we stop
to think on the
accident.

Think on our mistake.

This is not to say that
either is wrong.

When conversation
dwindles, that silence
does not have to
drown the space
it surrounds.

On Anticipation, For A Feeling That Comes On Sparingly

The space between days is a draft come
in below your toes in the middle of the
night. The reaching there between them,
the search for the source.

Finding all the windows to be closed.
Not knowing where else to look.
Falling asleep, intruded upon.

When you wake to humid air and unturned
sheets, the body folds into its own murmur.
You are compelled to find yourself in
your own hands, where you know you
no longer live.

Finding all the house to be empty.
Not knowing where else to look.
Getting dressed, the hollow sound.

On a street corner three blocks away
a man is hit while crossing the street.
It very well could have been you.
It very well could have been the last
person you spoke to.

The space between the days where the
rooms feel un-watched, where the air
from outside does not try to crawl
inside of you, where you do not feel
enveloped by the kind of howl a building
makes when you are alone inside of it.

You do not remember if you locked the door.

Making Sense Of What You Are Told To Be

You know
you are meant
to love but
how does a
sharp tooth
not catch on
the loose pieces of
a soft thing?

A Body Made From Separation

You are not given the body, but
you are asked to inhabit it.

Imagine a field with no space.
Imagine calling the sound someone
makes when they scream, a bell.

It is every single day, like a sink
full of dishes and a door that does
not lock. It is something under the
door, and going to sleep anyway.

You are not given the sky, but
you are told what it is meant to be.

What torture, to be told how
beautiful a thing is meant to be,
as you stare into its nonexistence.

What We Know We Must Inevitably Come To Be

You, of open mouth; you, made from back
when we still wore our hair down by
our shoulders; you, of smiles that ask
those looking to stay away.
You: the end given over to the means.

We come to know you.

Some place in a town no one you know has ever
been to, some person falls asleep next
to some other person. One got home later than
the other. Neither said goodnight.

You, in the corner. You, all
flooded
with "run."

There is a room of ladders, reaching upward, never
with long enough arms to find the place
they ache for. No one bothers pulling themselves
onto the body of the reaching things. No one
bothers to climb into the thing that
cannot, itself, reach that which
it desires. No one walks into this room.
It is not safe to come down.

It is not safe to imagine the
floor is not all made from nails.
You, uncome from yourself.
You, unraveled in the space
where there is no room.

We come to know you:
she who we wish to become.

Left Back

When a great thing
falls, it can be heard
by all those who once
looked up to it.

And what of the
human heart?

When the human
heart falls, it is told
to keep quiet.

When a human heart
breaks, the only thing
left is the footsteps
that once belonged to
an idea that once was
called by a name

A Monument Is Built To Something Beautiful, And Still, You Cannot Smile

What does it sound like if not all the
words that leapt, in one motion, inside
of you the first time you almost went
through with stepping out into traffic?

What does it feel like if not claustrophobia
and isolation baring their teeth to one
another and finding how similar their
sharpness looks?

What does it look like if not
mistaking a distant forest fire
for the sunset?

What can we ask but
to be
spared?

Alien

They ought to be
like magic -
they ought to take
something
from inside of you
that seems
to be of another
world.

They ought to wrap
it around their
hands, weave it
through their
fingers, something
to always
hold them,

something to
always be held
by them.

On Things That Cannot Be Avoided

If you apologize
to the ground for
the way you step,

she will never
be able to hold you
right.

She will not be
able to do the thing
she does best.

It wears on her,
heavy. A reminder
that her open arms
go unseen.

Something Like Advice, For Those Who Did Not Ask
pt. 3

Where We've Gone

Come Home to yourself.

Do I mean to say,
come to the street you
were born on.

Do I mean to say,
come to the hands
who begged for you.

Did I mean to say,
the sun does not know
a world without light.

From The Wreckage: A Beacon

Sometimes, when it
howls, it is only the
wind. Sometimes,
it has teeth. Wisdom
is being able to hear
the difference.

A Heart Like Dirty Dishes

Be a gone thing,
if you must;

saturated with
the sound made
by empty hands.

Do not fear the
noise of a scream.

Find a way to
keep from
scaring yourself
away.

What They Do Not Tell You About Bringing Yourself Back To Life

Breathe so that you
may be certain that
you are not submerged.
In the same way, Love,
with ferocity, so that
you may be certain that
you are not empty.

For The Ones That Must

They call the thing that
fights to keep itself, rageful.

So, we show them that storm.
Show them what it tastes
like to be made the way
we are.

Be rageful.
Do not let yourself be
shamed for refusing to
be drowned.

She Tells Me She Has Found Someone Whose Heart Cannot Beat For Her, She Tries To Pound It Alive

Untangle yourself from
the bodies of the dead.
They will not wake, no
matter how long you
lie with them. They may
touch you, and they
may crawl inside of you,
but what is dead cannot be
loved awake; what has
rotted cannot be healed. You
are no grave, your body
no tombstone.

This Grave is Nothing but a Lonely Home, So We Give Her Water and Keep Her Safe

Take the grave they
gave you, climb into
its hollow heart,
plant the flowers
and watch them grow.
From where you are
meant to meet your
end, let there be
new beginnings.

The Fear of Being Torn Into

When a thing tells you it is soft,
You will watch it bare its teeth
and be still. You will think, "soft
things do not bite." It will
growl and snarl, and you will
be still. Soft things do not break
skin. When you watch the mouth,
a gradient of skin and spit
and red, unhinge, it will not cross
your mind that it is your blood
dripping from its chin.

You do not have to encounter
this thing without flinching. Do not
feel guilty for failing to trust the
thing that hurts you. You do
not have to be still once you
know what it is capable of.

You are not obligated to go back
to "how is your mother"
conversation; you do not have
to indulge that which makes
you bleed.

They have already taken their
share; give them no more.

Expand, Expand, Expand

Do not do your body the
disservice of shrinking
yourself down to make
others more comfortable.
The universe likes her
stars explosive.

Be Careful for One Another, We Are Made From the Same Stuff

Do not bite it
until it cracks,
sit with it
until it hatches.

For The Sky To Move

girl, mighty and
impenetrable, let
yourself be open.

let it be uprooted,
the surface
scratched at.

let yourself be caught
beneath the nails of
those who cannot
grow you back.

trust that you can
survive, unprotected.
trust that you are
strong enough to
feel, uncovered.

We Do Not Gape, But We Yearn.

You must never
let go of the thing
that makes the
open parts of you
feel like doors,
rather than wounds.

When You Hear What Sounds Like Knocking.

Do not bury yourself to protect your heart.
All that pressure cannot go unfelt; leading
others to believe that you are dead will
not make that claustrophobia feel like home.
You are so much more alive than the thing
crawling inside of your chest would have
you believe. That knocking is coming from
inside of you; it is trying to tell you your name.

How To Tear Yourself Into Pieces And Still Call Yourself The Same Thing You Were Before

cut the sheets into pieces.
when they fuck you, take it as a promise.
replace the word "fuck" with "love." you will make less sense to
everyone but yourself.
dare yourself to drink the whole bottle. let yourself down.
ask the sink to keep your secrets. she will comply. get the sink replaced.
force out all the creases in your clothing. call the smooth things new.
tell them you taste salt when they offer you sugar.
stop talking about your heart. no one else can see it. it is suspension of
disbelief, for them to take your word for it when you say it is there. no
one cares if it is there.
keep talking about your heart. who gives a fuck if people are listening. let
them see the glow of it coming from your throat when you speak of
your great capacity for what they cannot fathom into words. glow, like
you are convincing them of something.
sometimes people will tell you that you have done a good job without
seeing what it is you have done.
it is easier for them to go on if they do not pay attention to the things
you put your life into. it takes too much effort to care.
when he stops saying it first, stop saying it first. see how long it takes
before he realizes. pay attention. what happens next is important.
leave the clothes outside to dry, even though last time they were stolen.
imagine that there are not freezing cold days where the sky is still full of
the sun.
imagine that one thing could really keep you warm, all the time.
imagine that you never have to do it for yourself. imagine no one else
has to do it for you.
imagine you are warm, all on your own.

On Pleasing The Moon, As Its Daughter

The moon has no space to weep
because she is always being
watched, from somewhere,
through telescopes with
people on the other side looking
through them that expect her
to be magnificent and alien and
unfamiliar. Pain is too familiar.
If we looked at the moon and saw
her acknowledging her own
isolation, how quickly I imagine
we would lose interest in her.
We were taught: "no one
marvels at miserable things."
We learned young, these bodies,
beneath skin like the moon, were not
born to be marveled at.

This is not the end.